About the author

Muriel Freeborn was ninety years old when she began her book, *Ellie Hopeson 91* in 2017. Inspired by the life of a friend, who had been a writer, and had recently died, her writing proved to be therapeutic and an unexpected pleasure. She is interested in making music with friends, and is a member of her local church. She lives in Wiltshire. She has written for the elderly and the very elderly, and also for the young, who will be elderly one day.

ELLIE HOPESON 91

Muriel Freeborn

ELLIE HOPESON 91

Vanguard Press

VANGUARD PAPERBACK

© Copyright 2018
Muriel Freeborn

A CIP catalogue record for this title is
available from the British Library.

ISBN 978 1 784655 08 2

*Vanguard Press is an imprint of
Pegasus Elliot MacKenzie Publishers Ltd.*
www.pegasuspublishers.com

First Published in 2018

**Vanguard Press
Sheraton House Castle Park
Cambridge England**

Printed & Bound in Great Britain

Acknowledgments

Bath Library for helpful information.

Bradford on Avon Library for help in photocopying.

Go Get Organised Bath for typing the manuscript.

Dedication

Dedicated to Jean Bellamy

Chapter 1

Ellie Hopeson knew she was old, she had been getting old for quite a time. Her hair had turned grey several years ago, just as her mother's hair had done when she was sixty. Ellie didn't think that made her old, nor did she take too much notice of the way her face had grown thinner, and its lines more pronounced – she was just getting old.

She had lived on her own for over twenty years since her husband passed away, managing to deal with the strains and stresses of keeping an old house watertight and in good order, and managing to keep her small garden tidy and colourful.

She had gone down with a cold, and had been off colour for several days, to be followed by a persistent cough which seemed reluctant to go.

The realisation that she was old came to her when she was on the mend and feeling better in herself and able to shop in town. She had never overloaded her basket, preferring to shop frequently, but now, on her way home, she was surprised how slowly she was walking. Never one to dawdle, she found herself being passed briskly by other shoppers. She was grateful for a rest when she had to wait for the lights to change at the zebra crossing. She found herself pleased to stop and give way when room was tight for an oncoming pushchair.

Yes, she had been told at her local health centre that her blood pressure was higher than it should be, and help was given for that, but for her age she was reasonably fit.

Old or not, she had no thought of moving from her home, despite the occasional problems, she loved living where she was. Where would her son and his family sleep if she moved into a small flat? She loved their visits, however infrequent they were… the grandchildren's lives of work, gave them little time to drive the hundred odd miles to see her. She understood that.

So Ellie settled down, accepting the restrictions which were sensible if she wanted to avoid the pitfalls which came through not taking care of herself. She was thankful she was still able to look after herself, shop and cook simple meals, and now often depending on the pre-prepared variety she could buy so easily. Her gardening had become pottering, but nevertheless, she enjoyed doing what she could do, and was thankful for each day that dawned. She was sad when her son's wife had died, leaving him a widower on the verge of his retirement, but his children had married, and started families themselves, which was a comfort for him. He visited her as often as he could, and phoned too.

She thought to herself, with some amusement, that in her younger days, satisfaction came in the completion of the marking of a pile of school books, and the arriving back to school after an outing with her class. Now she found satisfaction in preparing a meal for herself and washing up afterwards, to say nothing of sorting out her refuse sacks and bins for the Monday morning collection. The completion of everyday tasks gave her a certain peace of mind and she could in all conscience sit down and watch television any time during the day.

The years of entertaining had ended, not the passing away of friends whom she entertained and who entertained her over the years, now she doubted her ability to be a good hostess, she could run to a cup of tea or a cup of coffee, and she was delighted when the occasion arose. Family visits were an occasion to dine out, and that was a great pleasure.

It was at night that she did feel a lack of company. Of an evening she had watched television, gone to bed at a reasonable hour, and with a bit of luck, gone straight to sleep. Perhaps it was because of her age – it was said that as one got older, one didn't need so much sleep – that she found herself lying awake until the early hours of the morning. She was tired, but found herself thinking of times long ago, and people she had once known would come to mind, for no apparent reason, quite out of the blue. She would lie in a state of dozing, unsure as to whether or not she had been to sleep at all.

She did start to wonder what would happen to her if she could no longer look after herself. She supposed that she would follow in the path of her friends, and retire to a rest home, where she would be grateful that she was cared for when she could be no longer active. Sometimes, when Ellie lay awake, she would evaluate her life – she considered herself a good person. She had taught young children and devoted herself to her family. She would not leave any great accomplishments behind her, she came to the conclusion she wouldn't really leave any mark at all! She realised that life was unfair at times, some ended up with more than others. She watched the news on television every day, a legacy from the war years she supposed. She liked to know what was happening regarding the political scene here, and in the world generally. She was also interested in people's behaviour to each other. She was aware of individuals who committed dreadful crimes against their fellow human beings. She wondered if criminals ever paid the price for their crimes if they escaped justice. Those who made millions of pounds at the expense of the young, drawn into drug taking, and those who profited at the expense of others who were insecure and vulnerable. She hoped that none of her 'children' took such a path.

The arrival of a new neighbour was a pleasant distraction, another single lady, much younger than herself. She was friendly towards Ellie right from the day she moved in, and responded to Ellie's note of welcome through her letterbox. Ellie found her an easy relaxed person, and the two women were seen conversing happily in a way that was not overfamiliar. Ellie was grateful for that, as she tended to be a rather private person. Talking of ailments, however minor, she found displeasing. It seemed to be that people of her age always had plenty to talk about on that subject, not that she was unsympathetic where others were concerned, she just found it difficult to talk about herself. She was quite willing for her neighbour, Bea, to exchange house keys in case of emergencies, something she had done with her previous neighbour. There was nothing worse than to find oneself locked out, as neither house had a back entrance, being in an old terrace of four houses, situated directly on the main road in their small country town. It was useful too, for them to have a distinctive bell ring. Ellie was always cautious when someone rang her doorbell and she wasn't expecting anyone! She did use the "spy glass" her son had fitted for her to make sure the caller remained at the bottom of her steps after ringing. She also had a security bar which allowed her to open her door a fraction. Even so, she was pleased to be able to identify her new neighbour without any concern.

The autumn days of her ninety-first year, after the clocks had been changed to their fall-back time, and the curtains were drawn in late afternoon, found her sitting and listening to the news on the television. Her old fingers were becoming stiff and it made her lifelong hobby of knitting and embroidery difficult for her.

Ellie thought of the tangled mess the world seemed to have got itself into, she felt a deep concern for the future her grandchildren would inherit. Would that she was able to come back and see how they were getting on! She smiled to herself, as she supposed that was what all parents wished when they were coming to the end of their lives. Ellie wasn't one to have deep religious convictions, but she did always wonder if the good and the bad reaped the same after death. She changed the programme from the news.

"Oh dear," she mused, "do all old people have these thoughts?" And she got up from her chair, went into her kitchen and made a cup of tea.

Ellie found herself looking out from her bedroom window when she closed her curtains as daylight faded. She liked to reassure herself that Bea was at home, as she could just see that her light downstairs was on. The people living the other side of her were often away. They were fairly new residents too, and apart from an early introduction, she saw little of them. She was surprised how much a comfort it was for her to have Bea living next door.

Chapter 2

Late one evening Ellie was sitting in front of her television, half dozing, half watching the TV news programme, waiting for the moment she felt a real desire to climb the stairs to bed, when there was a ring at her front door. It was Bea.

She threw back her rug, and being careful not to overbalance, she went slowly to her front door. She didn't put her light on, just in case it wasn't Bea after all. Looking through her spy-glass she could see her neighbour dimly, standing at the bottom of her steps. Ellie didn't hesitate to open her door. "Bea," she said showing her surprise, "are you all right?"

"Yes, I am," replied Bea. "I saw that your light was still on and I wondered if you were well. It is very late and long past the time when you usually retire to bed. It is past midnight."

"I find it difficult to sleep sometimes," Ellie confessed. "I watch television until I feel really sleepy, then I hope I will drop off quickly when I get into bed. It doesn't always work though."

"Put your coat on and we will walk round the block, it isn't cold tonight."

Ellie was hesitant, it wasn't the kind of thing she did late at night, but her friend was very persuasive and in her sleepy mental state she did not like to say 'no'. Before she could decide whether or not it was sensible to be going out this late, she found herself putting on her coat and slipping her key into her pocket. She closed her front door, putting her arm in Bea's arm, and letting her new friend lead her along the dry pavement. The street lights were still on and a half moon shone in a sky with a few clouds to keep it from view for long. It was a quiet peaceful night, with no traffic, Ellie noted.

She was surprised how wide awake she felt now that she was out in the fresh air. Instead of keeping to the pavement, Bea turned aside leading Ellie through a small gate into the local park. Every so often a tall lamp illuminated their path as it curved this way and that around the bushes and between the trees. Their slow pace and Bea's steady arm induced an unexpected peace in Ellie.

As they progressed towards a distant council light, Ellie became aware that they were walking towards a group of people moving amongst themselves, seemingly going nowhere. She heard a rattling sound, and as they approached, she saw in the dim light that each figure wore a long coat which was covered in an assortment of loosely hanging objects. There were bunches of keys, necklaces, handbags of various sizes, and even small clocks. They were arranged so closely that there was no question of the figures being able to sit down. With heads bowed and shoulders bent, they moved in great weariness, taking no notice of Ellie and Bea.

"Who on earth are they?" whispered Ellie as they moved aside to avoid them.

"Thieves," said Bea, and after a moment she added, "it's their choice."

So distracted was Ellie by what she had seen, she made no further comment, but deep in thought she wondered where such a collection had come from, and from whom they had been taken. They walked on in silence.

As they rounded a bend in the path, ahead of them Ellie could see another light, it flickered as the branches of the nearby trees moved slowly in a slight breeze. On approaching it they saw that another group of figures seemed to be moving round and round as the other group had done. At first Ellie wasn't sure whether or not they were even people. She felt Bea leading her off the path to avoid close contact with them. Ellie looked across at them as they passed, she could see that one figure was carrying another who was the larger of the two, and that the carrier was extremely weary, not being able to rest.

When they were well past the disturbing scene, Ellie ventured to ask Bea about what she had seen.

"The old men, who were carrying the others, had abused and mistreated both men and women in their lives, and until they showed remorse for what they had done, there was no rest for them," explained Bea.

Ellie was silent. She followed wherever Bea led, hardly conscious of the direction of their walk, whether or not she was cold or tired.

Bea broke the silence. "Time we went home, Ellie," she said, changing direction. Their path led them around the edge of the playing field Ellie recognised, where she had often watched football and cricket being played. She was just glad that her outing was coming to an end. She was not expecting to see any more strange gatherings, and she quickened her pace in response to Bea's call for home.

As they rounded the green, coming towards them were other walkers, walking on the grass, avoiding the path, following one behind the other. The night had darkened and the individuals could not be seen clearly. What was odd, though, was the fact that each was carrying a hand mirror into which they were all looking. None strayed from the line which, as far as Ellie could see, had no visible end. The two women reached the park gate and stepped out onto the pavement. Glancing back, Ellie was conscious of the line of walkers stretching around the whole perimeter of the green.

"They had no time in their lives for anyone but themselves," said Bea in response to Ellie's questioning look.

"Are they going to do that for ever?" asked Ellie.

"Probably," replied Bea, "unless they can feel compassion for someone, then I expect they will be able to move on."

Almost as soon as Bea had spoken they reached their respective front doors. Ellie put her hand in her coat pocket and drew out her key. Saying 'goodnight' and thanking Bea for her company, she let herself in. Once in the hall she was overcome by a deep sense of fatigue –

going upstairs was an impossibility. She steadied herself on the bannisters and began to walk down the hall to her chair in the dining room. In her tired state she became aware that the hall seemed to be longer than she remembered it. She began to be fearful that she wouldn't be able to get to the end, indeed it seemed to be leading her into an unfamiliar place altogether. She put out her hand and grasped something in front of her...

Chapter 3

The central heating came on at seven thirty. The boiler was in the kitchen just feet away from where Ellie sat motionless in her armchair. The little explosive noise it made brought her to consciousness. She found herself still and uncomfortably cold. She tried to bring the rug further up to cover her shoulders, but without success. She would have to get up – nature called. She turned off the blank television and moved slowly to her downstairs toilet. Her mind clung to the impression that she had been in the park and seen very strange scenes the night before. It was vague in her mind and eager to slip away. The details of how she came to be out at night quite escaped her. She felt that she had been walking with someone, but she had no recollection as to who it was. She couldn't remember looking at them. *How very odd it was*, she thought. *It must have had something to do with the story on the television news I was watching yesterday*. She sat quietly, still feeling sleepy.

The next thing she knew was a ring on her front doorbell, and recognised her neighbour's signal. She rose slowly, Bea would wait for her to open the door.

"Hello, Ellie," she said, seeing Ellie up and dressed. "I am pleased you are all right. I noticed that your downstairs light was on in the middle of the night when I went downstairs for a cup of water. It was still on when I looked again this morning."

"I must have gone to sleep in the chair," confessed Ellie, realising that she could not have been out, but had dreamed the disturbing episode.

"What time is it?" she asked.

"Well, it is past nine o'clock."

"Do come in," said Ellie, opening the door wider. "It is cold out there."

"I will for a minute, I also wanted to tell you that I shall be going away for a few days to visit my younger sister up north. She lives near Edinburgh with her husband and family."

"How very nice for you," said Ellie, leading her friend into her dining room, which was just beginning to get warmer.

"Yes," continued Bea, "we have always been close, and it was a bit of a shock for me when her husband was offered a job in Edinburgh and they moved so far away from me."

"My sister lived in Australia. She went there years ago when I was in my twenties and I am afraid we rather lost touch," said Ellie regretfully.

"That is really sad," continued Bea. "It doesn't take me long to fly to Edinburgh from here, my sister and her husband meet me at the airport."

"I have never flown in an aeroplane," admitted Ellie, "and I don't suppose I ever will now. When do you leave?" she asked.

"I go the day after tomorrow, and I shall be away for two weeks," more than her usual few days, she realised.

"Let me have your contact number – just in case," said Ellie.

"I will do that," said Bea on her way out.

When her friendly neighbour had gone, and the front door had closed leaving Ellie alone with her thoughts, she climbed the stairs slowly to wash and change her crumpled clothes. Her double bed had not been slept in. She sighed to herself, and wished she could have shared her odd dream with her husband, Norman. She was aware that she missed him, but she did not like to keep thinking of the past, keeping her mind on the present helped her to cope with daily life more easily. There were a hundred and one demands for her attention apart from shopping, watching appointments, remembering birthdays, keeping abreast of the many communications which came through the letterbox each day, and of course, remembering to change her library book before passing the 'due back' date.

She moved on to the bathroom realising that she would miss Bea. A fortnight seemed a long time for an empty house next door. Although she was reluctant to take a holiday on her own now, she thought it would be lovely to stay in a comfortable hotel for a few days.

Preparing a late breakfast in her kitchen, her thoughts moved to Bea and her visit to stay with her sister. That in turn, as she sat eating her breakfast, brought to mind her own sister, Patricia. Had she made enough effort to keep in touch with her? She felt she had hardly known her, it must have been seventy years at least since she last saw her.

Chapter 4

"Oh! Do let her have it for a while, for goodness sake."

Ellie's mother was becoming impatient with both her daughters as they squabbled over the knitted doll Ellie had been given.

Their Auntie Lorna had been to visit for the day, and had brought the knitted doll for Ellie, and a teddy bear for Patricia.

Minnie Sparkes always tried to make the visits of her unmarried sister a happy time for her, as they were a special break from caring for their mother, who, a widow in her sixties, had become increasingly poor sighted. Minnie, being married and having the two girls and husband, Bob, to look after, had her hands full. Lorna, her elder sister, did domestic work in the district as a part-time job, fitting it in with her mother's needs. Hers was a life of caring for others, which began when her father was killed in an accident at work. Her mother had suffered greatly from the shock. She was awarded a small pension, and so old Sarah and her elder daughter lived quietly together.

It was when Auntie Lorna went home from her visit, that the girls started their squabbling. Patricia, younger by only eighteen months, was very dismissive of her teddy bear and took a great fancy to Ellie's doll. Trying to prepare a cooked meal for her husband and sort out the girls, was taking all of Minnie's patience. They often fell out, and Minnie usually had to rely on the older child's softer nature to give in to Patricia's requests.

"She's younger than you are, Ellie, and not so understanding. Let her borrow the doll for a few minutes, you can play with teddy."

Ellie knew the 'few minutes' her mother suggested would last until Patricia was fast asleep in bed before she would be able to take possession of her doll. Her mother often told her that she was a big girl now that she had started school, and being kind and helpful would please her teacher, whom Ellie adored. The result was Ellie, more often than not, did what her mother asked when it concerned her paddy-prone sister.

"When Patricia is four, she will be going to school, and will learn to be more understanding when it comes to other children's toys," Minnie explained to her, hoping that school would be more successful in curbing her younger daughter's demanding behaviour.

Keeping a calm and quiet house was Minnie Sparkes's main concern for when her tired husband, Bob, came in from work. Patricia's tantrums were enough to drive most people out of earshot. Bob Sparkes did his best to divert his younger daughter from whatever it was that had upset her, but Minnie's aim was to have two quiet well behaved girls ready to greet their father at the end of his day.

Really, the two girls could not have been more different in regard to their characters. Ellie had been a perfect baby, sailing through her early years without fuss, putting up with her fractious younger sibling who had needed a great deal of attention from their mother. It was a case of when Patricia was good, she was very good, and when she was not – well, enough said. She certainly had a mind of her own and all the confidence in the world, as they say. She couldn't wait to get to school and be a 'big girl' like her sister, Ellie.

Both girls were very fond of their Auntie Lorna who gave them her full attention whenever she visited her sister. Attractive and kindly, Lorna had yet to meet her man. Her mother hinted now and then that she hoped one day her daughter would find a wise young man. Lorna secretly agreed with her mother, although she kept her thoughts to herself and just smiled when her mother mentioned it. At her age she felt spinsterhood approaching if Mr Right did not turn up soon. Her sister, Minnie, had been most fortunate to marry Bob Sparkes, but Lorna saw that some marriages could be less than harmonious. And besides, she thought, her mother needed her, and she often told her how grateful she was that her daughter looked after her. Indeed, old Sarah had always been devoted to her two daughters, and they in turn were devoted to their widowed mother.

Patricia's exuberant behaviour continued as she grew up. She was as lively at school as she was at home, although the constraints at school, where good behaviour was insisted upon, often resulted in her showing her frustrations when she arrived home. She was a popular girl, and had many friends who sought her lively company. She was fortunate in having understanding parents who pacified her when she thought anyone had been unfair towards her. She knew she was loved at home, if, for whatever reason, she felt unloved by the friend of the moment.

Ellie, on the other hand, progressed through school in a quieter manner. She worked studiously to attain good marks, as she wanted to become a teacher, which meant going to college once her school days were over. Ellie also had a strong character, fairness in dealing with others was important to her too, but she was less impulsive than her sister, altogether steadier, and more careful not to rush into things without due thought.

Chapter 5

Going to bed quite late again, Ellie was pleased to see that her neighbour, Bea, was home after visiting her sister in Edinburgh. Bea's bedroom light shone into her garden and was a beacon of comfort to Ellie. Her days had passed, as they tended to do now, with nothing out of the ordinary happening. She had missed Bea's cheerful greeting as they met coming and going on their respective trips to the local shops. Sometimes they stopped for short exchanges, to comment on local affairs which interested them both, like whether or not they approved of the council's plans for more housing, a frequent topic of conversation in the town. It would be nice, thought Ellie, to invite Bea in for a cup of tea to hear all about her trip to Scotland.

Ellie had recently engaged a domestic help – she found hoovering exhausting – she didn't make much mess, she was by nature a tidy person, but dirt would appear and dust would settle, and her eyes were still sharp enough to see it.

It was when Dorothy arrived with her cleaning equipment, doing as much as she could in her one hour, that Ellie sat quietly, supposedly reading her newspaper. In fact, Dorothy's coming on a regular basis reminded her of her dear Auntie Lorna who helped elderly people in a similar way. And those thoughts in turn reminded her of her grandmother, Sarah. Sarah had passed away just after the war when Ellie was eighteen and preparing to go to teacher training college. The family had struggled through the war years, with blackouts, rationing, following the news avidly on the radio.

By the time the war was finally over, Ellie's Auntie Lorna was working in her domestic capacity at the Municipal Buildings in their town. Her sister, Minnie, Ellie's mother, shared in caring for their frail mother, Sarah.

It was the time too, when Ellie was accepted as a student for teacher training, that the pattern of life changed for the family. How well she remembered those days, thought Ellie.

The first surprise came with the news that Auntie Lorna was getting married. Ellie remembered phoning home from her college shortly after she had settled to her studies, to hear the news from her mother. How she wished she could return home immediately and meet the new uncle who had captured her auntie's heart. Ellie's mother had been overjoyed at her sister's news. She deserved her happiness after the years of care and devotion to their mother. So George Somerset entered the family and carried off the young girls' auntie to set up home with him. Would that her grandmother had lived to see her elder daughter married, sighed Ellie to herself.

With clothes rationing still in place and austerity still the norm, George and Lorna married quietly in the registry office. They chose a time during the spring of the year when Ellie and Patricia were on holiday from college and school.

They gathered with a few friends they both knew from their work at the Municipal Offices where they had met, it was a very happy occasion.

George's first wife had died during the war, they had been unable to have children. George had found Lorna an indispensable friend and confidante. Everyone who knew them were delighted when Lorna accepted George's hand in marriage.

Ellie often remembered those days, as she sat keeping out of the way when Dorothy was cleaning. Family life was never the same after the war. People's attitude changed. Some hoped for a new beginning, a different direction, a life of more opportunities – more personal freedom. For Ellie change did come, not gradually, but in an unexpected jolt.

Chapter 6

It was bravado really that made the girls at school vie with each other as to who had done it. Some could be believed, of course, and some joined in so as to be thought modern and part of the social scene, where barriers were breaking down now peace had finally come. Patricia, and girls in the sixth form at school, met in a huddle, talking over their evenings out at the local dances, held most Saturdays. The young girls, growing up fast, were beginning to use lipstick, paint their nails and perm their hair, eyes firmly fixed on the boy of the moment.

Patricia had decided that when she left school, as soon as possible, if she had her way, she would take a course of shorthand and typing and work in an office. Her mother and father supported her in this, as they realised Patricia was not destined to enter the teaching profession as her sister planned to do, and the other avenue in becoming a nurse was definitely not to Patricia's liking. Shorthand and typing seemed to have a glamour about it – working with an office team appealed to her. She would have to dress smartly and could use lipstick and paint her nails – she would meet the opposite sex. With a salary, she could afford to go to the pictures and be lifted into the adult world. And so, at the end of the school year and approaching seventeen, Patricia enrolled into the local secretarial college. Minnie and her husband, Bob, were proud of their girls. Relaxing in the post war years, despite the restrictions that were still in place, they began to enjoy life.

Patricia's friends from school continued to meet up, although, as they grew older, it was individual friendships which developed. The girls had boyfriends whom they met at the local dances which remained very popular, and those who were not keen on dancing, queued for the cinema – its back seats for choice. Patricia kept her social life private where it concerned her boyfriend of the moment. Her parents were aware that she kept in touch with her school friends, one or two of them visited their home and had been known to Minnie and Bob for several years. The boys they didn't meet. Minnie and Bob were young once and knew the boundaries of good behaviour before marriage. They had told Patricia that it was perfectly in order for her to bring a boyfriend home to meet them. If they happened to live nearby, it was quite possible for them to know the parents.

After the end of the war, men were still called up for 'war service', or National Service it was generally called. Young lads of seventeen were liable to be sent overseas. It was a wrench for them to leave home, and even to be away for eighteen months seemed like a lifetime for the young adults. Farewells were painful.

For Ellie there was no opportunity to meet the opposite sex. The college rules forbade any contact, gates were locked soon after supper, so night-time escapades for trainee teachers were out of the question. Students were there to work and study, any breach would prove one's unsuitability for the profession.

Ellie enjoyed her college life, the opportunity for making friends of like minds, and the experience of lectures and study, and it gave her the chance to practise her teaching skills. All too soon her course came to an end, and Ellie joined the staff at a school some distance from home. She boarded with a single lady during the week and bussed home at the weekends.

When Ellie arrived home one Friday evening, she was surprised to find her Auntie Lorna and Uncle George visiting. There were solemn faces all round and the greeting Ellie received was decidedly muted. After leaving her weekend bag in her bedroom, she hurried down the stairs to hear what had brought about the family gathering. Even Patricia was sitting quietly watching the four adults with their glum expressions.

At first nobody spoke. Ellie thought someone must have died, so she sat quietly. The silence in the room was only broken by the tick of the clock on the mantelpiece. Ellie had not realised how loud it was. Obviously there had been a conversation of importance before she had arrived, and someone had to repeat to her what had been said. Finally, her mother addressed her, and explained that Auntie Lorna and Uncle George were considering emigrating to Australia.

Chapter 7

When Lorna agreed to marry George Somerset, it was discussed as to where they would live. For a short while, both decided that it was sensible to remain in the house George had shared with his first wife, until they had formed their future plans. In marrying again, and, as George put it, 'starting afresh', he no longer felt comfortable with so many things about the house which he and his first wife had chosen together, on the other hand, Lorna was not altogether happy living in the house George had made his home with somebody else. The decision to move was agreed, the question was, how far away would they have to go before the past was in the past? Then, quite out of the blue, George overheard a conversation at work, a colleague was emigrating to Australia to begin a new career, taking advantage of the ten pound ticket scheme. The thought of going to Australia played on George's mind throughout the day, and when he and Lorna were at home after work, he put the proposition to her. Lorna could see that he was serious about the idea, and had replied that it would be interesting to find out more about it. Consequently, with guidance from the chappie at work, George applied to Australia House for details.

The urgency of the matter came when it was discovered that the ten pound scheme was for those under forty-five, and both George and Lorna were in their early forties. They had to decide quickly.

Ellie's mother, Minnie, was the one who was the most upset about their news. She and Lorna had always been close, their bond with their mother had been a strong one. Minnie had grieved deeply when she died. Lorna had found an unexpected love in George, and had passed through the loss of their mother more easily.

Minnie had also been feeling the growing away of her daughters. Patricia, coming and going in her own little world, Ellie, now living mainly away from home. Minnie could do without family disruptions, her close family was all her life. Her sister going off to Australia was hard to contemplate. When would she see her again? Keeping in touch would mean the occasional letter with perhaps a photograph. That would be all she could look forward to. On the other hand, Minnie felt that she could not make any parting too unbearable for Lorna, if that was what she really wanted to do. She would need to control her deep feelings and lean heavily on her husband, Bob, the ever sensible and loving Bob.

When Ellie thought back on those days, she realised how hard it must have been for her mother, and the inexplicable events that happened soon after that initial Friday afternoon meeting, when the family gathered to be informed of the decision to emigrate, left Ellie stunned, even to this day.

Living away from home for most of the week, Ellie felt cut off from the fallout of the news of the emigration to

Australia of her Auntie Lorna and Uncle George. She was sure that it was the main topic of conversation, as day after day Lorna kept her sister well informed about all the arrangements that had to be made.

It saddened Ellie to realise that there was also a growing distance between her and Patricia. Ellie felt a reluctance in Patricia to talk about their aunt's departure. When Ellie arrived home for the weekend, she met Patricia on the way out to meet up with her friends. Friendly in greeting, it seemed that her sister had other things to think about now that she was an independent woman, and the affairs of the family were best left with her parents. Ellie felt that she was watching events unfold from the sidelines.

Her parents wanted her to be comfortable and relaxed after her busy week teaching. Her mother, particularly, made every effort to remain cheerful, as she stressed that her sister's happiness was what mattered.

Even so, when Ellie recalled these days in her old age, she still felt there was an unsettled feeling in the house, and an enforced cheerfulness at times. She remembered the time when she returned home after a short holiday she had taken with a colleague. They had been to Wales where they could walk and enjoy the silence of the countryside, after the chatter and clatter of the classroom. She intended staying at home for the remainder of her holiday with her parents, who were not going away themselves, until Lorna and George had left for Australia. But it was a complete surprise and shock to her, when she heard that her sister, Patricia, was suddenly preparing to join her auntie and uncle in emigrating. Ellie remembered her announcement, saying that she was only going for two years, and then she would come home again. Her parents did not try to dissuade her from going. It would probably have been useless to try. It was all a long time ago, before Ellie was married. But she did find it difficult to understand Patricia's desire to emigrate when she knew how upset her parents would be at her leaving home to go so far away at the same time as her mother's beloved sister. It was tempting to think of Patricia as being selfish, although Ellie, like her parents, realised her confidence and eagerness to try something new drove her on to this exciting adventure.

After all, she would be a good companion for Auntie Lorna, and her aunt and uncle would keep an eye on her. That was a comfort for them. The family would wait patiently for her return.

But, of course, the inevitable happened. Patricia did not return after two years. She fell in love with a young Australian, and chose to settle out there permanently. During the following years, Minnie and Bob became proud grandparents and Ellie became an auntie. Lorna and George stood in for the English grandparents and made every effort in spoiling the new young family which came along.

Minnie would not travel to Australia to see her daughter and grandchildren. Her reason for not going was that she would not be able to say 'goodbye' to them once it was time to come home. She knew that they would only be able to afford to make the journey once – they would make do with phone calls, letters and photographs.

Chapter 8

Local boy, Norman Hopeson, was called to take up his National Service after he left school. He was a lively character, capable, sporty, and popular with his fellows, and in the army, where he was one of the recruits who were sent overseas. Tall and good looking, he enjoyed new experiences life had to offer him. He was considering staying in the army as a career, but to his dismay his life came to a sudden halt when he was involved in an accident on his motorbike. Speed was everything, and an unexpected obstruction in the road caught him unable to negotiate it and he came off his motorbike, breaking his ankle and his leg in the process. There had been a high wind the previous night and a branch had been ripped from a beech tree which was hidden from his view around a corner, and across the road.

He was fortunate in that the driver of a delivery van he had just overtaken, saw him seconds after his accident, and was able to help him. Other traffic had to stop and drivers were quick in helping to get Norman into the van and thence to hospital. He was very fortunate all round, he could have killed himself.

Thereafter, when all was eventually healed, he developed a slight limp, hardly perceptible, but more pronounced when he was tired. A career change was necessary, and he opted for teaching. He was a welcome student into the profession where his outgoing, cheerful personality was to his advantage. At that time training was reduced in order to fulfil the desperate need for teachers. Eventually, he took up a post in the school he had attended as a boy. He took advantage of living at home, helping his parents at the same time, as his younger brother was away at university and needed financial help.

Norman's ability soon saw him promoted to a deputy headship. There were many in the area who remembered him from his school days, and considered that he had done well.

In the way things happen sometimes, Minnie Sparkes, with more time on her hands, joined an evening class at the school where Norman taught in the daytime. She thought that she would like to learn dressmaking and make better use of a sewing machine originally belonging to her mother.

Norman's mother, Marion, also joined the class, and the two women struck up a friendship, comparing their respective efforts, commiserating and praising where appropriate. They both enjoyed talking about their families, one having two sons, the other two daughters.

Norman and Ellie's first meeting was when their parents socialised. Their fathers found a mutual interest in sport – Norman accompanied them to local football matches, sometimes going to the main league venues with them.

It wasn't long before the older couple planned a holiday together, which left Norman and Ellie seeking each other's company. For Ellie, Norman was a refreshing and likeable companion, and Norman appreciated Ellie's thoughtful and serious nature, able to voice her opinions in a clear, forthright manner, and, important for him, to be able to laugh at herself if she found she was becoming too dogmatic. Both their parents were delighted when the young people decided to get married.

How quickly those days had passed, Ellie thought as she rested in her chair, each one a mirror image of the other. Ellie stayed at home after her son was born until he was of school age when she returned to part-time supply teaching, standing in for staff who were ill or on maternity leave, it suited her very well.

Norman eventually obtained a headship, which meant that he was always busy.

All these days passed very quickly. One term flew by, followed by another, as did the years.

Did she appreciate her life then? Hum, she wondered. Even the passing of her parents, so sad at the time, was overtaken by the daily routine, and the effort of keeping abreast of things. There were highlights, of course, moments of excitement and moments of pride as son Brian did well at school.

And now, here she was, a widow in her old age, living far from her original home, where she and Norman had chosen for their retirement.

Her glancing back over the years was brief and fragmented, she found her day to day living, even with some domestic help, as much as she cared to cope with. There were still daily chores to attend to, and her own person to keep neat and tidy – looking after hair at hairdressers, teeth at the dentist, feet at the chiropodist – the list seemed endless at times.

She hesitated when fashion catalogues came through the letterbox, and she felt tempted to renew her wardrobe. Then again, she had plenty of clothes in good condition to 'last her out', as she thought to herself.

At the moment she was looking forward to the summer, the warm days when she would, with an effort probably, get the garden chair out from her shed, and sit outside in the shade of her apple tree, and read.

The thoughts that disturbed her most were those triggered by the daily news. In her youth she had no idea what was going on politically in other countries, what kind of government they had, and what their domestic problems were. The war had improved everyone's geography, and made the world more connected. The human species was proving itself just as cruel as in the much criticised dark and middle ages with their cruel behaviour. Today, she thought, was no different. That other world of punishment, in the beyond, must be growing as fast as the human population on earth. If only people said 'sorry', at least we could try to forgive. That is probably the hardest thing to do, she opined.

Chapter 9

A month or two later, when Ellie was again resting in her chair watching television after clearing away her supper things, and having laid out her cereal bowl and plate for breakfast the next day, her telephone rang. Someone selling something was her immediate thought. It wasn't her son Brian who always rang early each evening, unless, of course, it was something very important. She lifted the receiver and gave her number quietly.

"Hello, Auntie Ellie," a voice said, in a marked Australian accent, "this is Maisie Wheatley. How are you?"

"Goodness me," replied Ellie, in great astonishment. She quickly brought to mind that Maisie was Patricia's eldest daughter, and her niece.

"We are over here on holiday, and we would love to meet up," continued Maisie.

In the early days after Patricia had married and Ellie's parents were alive, the family had been in close contact. At least, Ellie's parents had, and Ellie had joined in when parcels were sent for birthdays and Christmas. After Minnie and Bob had died and Lorna and George had passed away too, communications became less frequent. Patricia's children had grown into adulthood.

They kept Ellie informed when Patricia became ill, and there was more contact at that time. After she had died, it was left to Christmas to keep the connection going.

It wasn't that Ellie didn't think about her sister, she did, but her own family life, her teaching and other interests dominated her thoughts for most of the time. It was only when Patricia had a birthday and again at Christmas that she came to feel in a more sisterly way. It must be said too, that Patricia, for her part, was wrapped up in her own family life, enjoying the closeness of her husband's Australian family, and in the early days, of her dear Auntie Lorna and Uncle George.

"We have hired a car whilst we are over here," said Maisie. "We've been to Scotland, and now we are driving southwards, staying for a day or two en route to see the well-known sites. John is interested in visiting castles. Now," she went on, "can we arrange to spend an afternoon with you as we make for the coast? We would so like to meet up if it is at all possible."

"Of course, of course," said Ellie, "I would love to meet you. How lovely of you to get in touch. You will have my address. I am very easy to find as I live in the centre of Rivermead. Let us decide on a day that will be convenient for you. It would be simply lovely to see you," said Ellie, warming at the prospect.

Nothing quite so exciting had happened in Ellie's life for a long time. Affection welled up inside her. All her sad recollection of her sister's emigration was overtaken by the thought of seeing her daughter, Maisie, and hearing first hand of the life her sister had led in Australia and of the family who were living on there. A date and time was arranged. Maisie and John would come for the afternoon in two days' time.

What news for Brian, she thought! He would not be able to join them at such short notice, but she would be able to tell him about their visit directly after they had gone.

With Dorothy's help, Ellie set about tidying the house to make it presentable for her niece and her husband. Dorothy kept the place clean at floor level, the litter of papers and magazines was Ellie's province for keeping orderly.

Ellie liked to have important reminder notes where she could see them, and sometimes an empty carton or tin left visible, to remind her to replace them the next time she went shopping. Some flowers would look cheerful and welcoming, she thought, as her mind went into overdrive to do all she could to make the visit memorable. Afternoon tea also required a decision – sandwiches and cakes, did Dorothy agree that would be suitable?

Ellie was surprised to find herself excited about the visit, pressure of long standing had suddenly been released. She couldn't help herself knocking at Bea's front door to tell her all about Maisie's visit. Bea offered to do anything required to help with the entertaining.

"All in hand, thank you, Bea," said Ellie.

"The weather forecast is for a fine day," Bea said, to help with the arrangements as best she could.

The day did dawn bright and sunny. Ellie made herself a light lunch, earlier than usual, so that she was able to rest and try to prepare herself calmly for when Maisie and her husband arrived. She knew they would find her house easily, and be able to leave their car in the car park of the town park which was just yards from Ellie's home.

Right on time the doorbell rang. Ellie didn't hesitate to open it with a rapturous greeting. She almost felt as if it was Patricia, come home, as Maisie, full of excitement too, stepped in to greet her Auntie Ellie. Husband John, close behind his wife, was more restrained in his introduction. He saw an elderly lady and was more gentle in his greeting.

Ellie led her visitors into her front room, tidily prepared for her Australian relatives.

At first, Maisie was full of their holiday in Scotland and the north of England. She explained to her aunt how they had saved for the holiday to celebrate John's retirement. Ellie let her lead the conversation, although Ellie was keen to hear about her sister, Patricia. She's just like her mother, thought Ellie, but not unkindly, the same bubbly outgoing nature.

Maisie was studying her English auntie as she talked, and saw her mother's sister as a very old grey-haired lady, a little on the frail side. The yearly Christmas greeting and birthday cards were a help in bridging the relationship gap. Now Ellie and her niece were touchingly close, and the family tie was strong. Ellie had seen the occasional photographs of her nieces as they grew up, but she didn't recognise her niece from those early days.

When Maisie and John had talked about the holiday they were enjoying, the conversation centred on the family. There was only second-hand contact between Maisie and her cousin, Brian. They had never met and their children had no knowledge of their second cousins, the gap was too wide, so mention of them was rather casual. Ellie was anxious to know more of her sister, Patricia. Who was her husband, Maisie's father? Was he successful? Had his family emigrated? So many questions Ellie wanted answered, also more detailed information of Patricia's illness.

She had known answers to some of her questions from her parents, as they had corresponded over the years, but many she had forgotten and wanted to be told again.

Maisie laughed and took out her iPad to show Ellie some pictures of where they now lived in Australia, for over the years the family had moved about.

There were early photographs of Patricia, she looked well and happy. There were some of the elderly Auntie Lorna and Uncle George . With a magnifying glass in her hand, Ellie was studying every detail in the photographs. She looked and looked in sheer delight.

Then, amongst the many passing in front of her, was one of an early family group. Ellie looked in disbelief, for there, standing at the back, was a tall, dark-haired handsome man who reminded Ellie of her husband, Norman, when he was young – pictures she had seen of him as a young teenager. She looked closely through the glass, saying nothing. Turning to Maisie, she asked who the handsome young man was.

"That's Jack," said Maisie.

"What relation is he to you then?" Ellie enquired.

"Ah well," replied her niece, an element of embarrassment creeping into her voice. "That's Mum's son she had before she married Dad. He's our stepbrother. He left home when he was eighteen and we have lost touch with him. Mum said he was a mistake when she was a teenager."

"Oh," said Ellie, looking intently at the youth again. Her own photographs on display were of her husband Norman in middle age and old age, but if Maisie had shown the same interest in them that Ellie was showing in Jack, she may have seen a certain likeness between them.

"I must put the kettle on," announced Ellie. "I am sure you would enjoy a cup of tea. You would, wouldn't you, John?" she said directing her attention to him.

"I would indeed," John replied.

And Ellie left them, wondering if the family photo she had seen was there by mistake. Maisie must have realised she had no knowledge of Jack. Ellie certainly could not remember any mention of Patricia's first born by her parents.

She busied herself making tea. Maisie came in to the kitchen to help carry in the sandwiches and cake, and left Ellie to bring in the tea trolley.

Cheerful as ever, the conversation covered many topics. Maisie knew little of her aunt's life as a teacher. John was keen to talk about his work in local government and Australian politics. They both said they enjoyed the connection with the Old Country and the visits to Australia of the Royal Family. Conversation returned to their holiday in the United Kingdom and they discussed where they would be heading next.

Ellie was prepared for their short visit and she understood that Maisie and her husband would want to visit as many places as they could before returning to Australia. It was unlikely that they would meet again.

At parting, Ellie gave Maisie a photograph of herself and Patricia when they were young children and Maisie reciprocated with a recent photograph of her family. Ellie said that she would pass it on to her son to remind him of his Australian relations.

And so, with a kiss and a hug they were gone, promising to keep in touch.

Chapter 10

Ellie returned to her front room where the empty cups and uneaten sandwiches and cakes were proof that she had entertained visitors. She sat, she just sat, for a while she was empty of all thought. She felt very tired and couldn't focus on any one thing. Thoughts began to race around in her mind after a while, pushing themselves up against each other, and not allowing anyone of them to have her full concentration and make sense. She closed her eyes and let one word sound from her lips.

"Jack," she said. The grandfather she didn't remember was called Jack. This Jack, who was he? Why was no mention of him ever made by Patricia? Did her parents know that Patricia had a baby boy before her two girls? Why was he so like her husband, Norman?

Ellie thought on. Was Patricia pregnant when she went to Australia? Was that the reason for her going and did she really want to go? Was her pregnancy the reason her parents did not persuade her not to go? Did they encourage her to go with Auntie Lorna and her husband? Was Jack's birth the reason her mother would not go to Australia?

Ellie could not help but to sit where she was, and try to find answers to this maze of questions leading her through these seemingly astounding revelations.

Then she came to the central point of why the young Jack in the photograph, now lost to her, was so like the young Norman whose early photograph she did have somewhere. How did Patricia know Norman anyway? Maisie said that her mother had told her that she became pregnant, after a party night, by someone she met. She had said no more than that.

Was Jack Norman's son? Was Norman, dashing and good-looking and full of life, responsible for this early slip before he went abroad on his National Service?

I can't ask, thought Ellie, *they are all gone*. Did Norman even know that he had made Patricia pregnant, did he even know who she was? Did Patricia know who he was at the time?

Then it dawned on Ellie that her sister must have known later on who her one-night lover was; it was obvious. When Ellie and Norman were married, Ellie sent a wedding photograph to her sister. It must have been a shock to Patricia to see a likeness between her brother-in-law and her own son. As Jack grew into his teenage years she could not have failed to see this even if she had not been aware at the time as to who had fathered her son. It was a secret she kept. *What family doesn't have secrets?* thought Ellie.

Did young Jack know who his father was? Had he seen the photograph of her wedding? It was quite likely that only Patricia knew the answers, but Ellie guessed her sister had been careful not to point out the likeness, and had it hidden away, or even destroyed the revealing photograph!

Thank goodness Auntie Lorna was there for her. She too must have seen the wedding photograph, as Ellie had sent one to her, and that would make her party to Patricia's secret. It would remain safe with Lorna who must have been thankful that she was in Australia away from awkward questions from her sister.

When the facts were beginning to make sense to her, Ellie began to consider how she thought she ought to react to it all. Throughout her life she had had a strong sense of what was right behaviour, of fairness and honesty. She found it unsettling that a relaxation in relationships was leading to many grey areas, and hard and fast rules of behaviour were not so clearly accepted. Perhaps it was always so, she thought, but now 'alternatives' were more visible. She guessed that her mother and father were very upset that Patricia had become pregnant in such a casual way – it had become their secret.

Ellie tidied away the tea things thinking sadly of her sister's son. Was he her nephew, or was he her stepson? Goodness only knew. She wondered where he was now. Was he still alive? Her heart went out to him. His parents, young, full of life after the war. Norman before his accident, preparing to leave home and serve in the peacetime forces, a handsome young man. And Patricia, excited to be able to be independent, just out of the restrictions of school life and unaware of the full consequences of finding out what sex was about.

To her surprise, Ellie found herself excusing them both, these things happened in families, she realised! Why not hers? It was in the past, long ago. Life was probably full of coincidences, even ones as improbable as this, thought Ellie. *I am too old*, she decided, *to let it worry me. It happened before I even met Norman*.

It must have been a very difficult time for her sister, for a while, as a single mother. She must have felt homesick and wanting to show her little boy to her parents. Ellie wished she could have put her arms around her and told her that it was all right, it was no major crime, and had even brought a smile to her lips. And her own parents must also have realised that their younger daughter's son resembled the Norman they had come to know, and had kept it to themselves until they died. But then, she thought, perhaps they had never seen a photograph of Jack either.

Ellie began to realise that forgiveness was the most important thing she could now do. To harbour ill will would destroy her piece of mind, but it didn't stop her thinking about her sister's behaviour.

The front doorbell rang, a timely interruption from Bea, her neighbour. Ellie struggled to her feet and slowly went to open the door.

"I saw that your visitors had gone," said Bea.

It wasn't being nosy, thought Ellie. *We live too close not to hear front doors closing along with loud farewells.*

"I've come to do the washing up. You must be really tired after all that excitement," said Bea.

"That is so kind of you, Bea," said Ellie gratefully. Time was when she would not have accepted help.

"I am exhausted," she continued. "It wasn't until they had gone that I realised just how tired I was."

"It won't take me a minute to wash up and put things away – you won't want it lying about until Dorothy comes again." And she set to work.

Chapter 11

Ellie was keen to tell her son, Brian, all about his cousin's visit. She planned to give him a phone call the same evening after she had finished eating the remaining sandwiches, and had strength enough to make herself a cup of decaffeinated coffee, but Brian forestalled her.

"Hello, Mum," he said brightly, "how did the visit go?"

"Hello, my dear. Do you know," she suddenly realised, "I am so tired that I really haven't enough energy to tell you all about it now. Is it possible for you to come at the weekend? A here and back in one day, just you, my dear." *I can't entertain*, she thought, *I can barely contemplate tea and biscuits*.

"Right," he said without hesitation, "will do. Next Sunday then, and I will take you out to lunch and you can tell me all about it."

The thought of lunch out suited Ellie just fine, but she would not relate all that had happened in a public place. It would be lunch first with a report on the pleasantries of their visit and only when they had returned home would she explain to him that he had two cousins in Maisie and her sister, and a half-brother in Jack. By then, she hoped she would have found some early photographs of his father, taken before they were married. She wished that she had the family photograph Maisie showed her, Brian would have to take her word for the fact that Jack was the image of his father at that age.

In the few days before the Sunday of Brian's visit, Ellie searched through some old family photograph albums and found the ones she was going to show Brian. Her son was more like her, but there were facial features similar to his father that were definitely of the Hopeson family. He wasn't quite as tall as his father was, and he was slightly more stocky. Both his parents were proud of his achievements in his becoming a solicitor. He had turned grey early, his mother always thought he looked distinguished because of it. He had no thoughts of re-marrying after his wife died, he kept himself busy with his work and was a keen gardener at home. He wasn't averse to the golf course where he met with friends from all walks of life. He was popular and outgoing, like his father was. With his mother's sister emigrating, his own two children and their families were his only relations of any closeness. He was finding himself more interested in his Australian relatives now that his cousins were also of the age of retirement and free to think of things other than work.

He was grateful that his mother was still alive and in reasonably good health, it made him a step away from being old himself. With his father gone and his wife's untimely death a few years ago, he did begin to feel the loss of family companionship.

Driving down the motorway on the arranged Sunday, he let his thoughts dwell on where he would like to settle when he finally did make up his mind to retire. His mother had a short time left to her in her own home, he thought. She had done well to manage, with a little help, in looking after herself, but she would tire of getting her own meals and also, mainly, of keeping her old house in good repair. There was always something which needed attention that he couldn't manage to do for her. Perhaps, he thought, she would settle nearer to him. For the moment he contented himself with the anticipation of hearing some interesting family news.

As for Ellie, she dressed in her best clothes for Sunday lunch with her son, a special occasion with or without the reason to impart family news. She was pleased at the interest Brian was taking in the visit of his Australian cousins. He had seen photographs of them in the past, sent to his mother by his Auntie Patricia, but it had only been a glance and a polite interest at the time. He knew his mother had sent some of him when he was young, and one of his marriage. It was a long time ago and family photographs tended to be put away in a drawer, and forgotten.

Lunch was enjoyed, more time eating than spent talking. Brian drove them home to continue their conversation without distractions. Seated comfortably, and both feeling like nodding off, they sat for a while in silence, eyes closing now and again, both aware that they wanted to enjoy each other's company and not spend their time together asleep in their chairs.

"I've something to tell you, Brian," announced his mother, in a tone of voice that made him open his eyes. "I didn't like talking about it over lunch, but I asked you down especially to tell you of some quite interesting and important family news."

Brian leant forward in his chair and stared at his mother with curious attention.

"Your cousin, Maisie, showed me a photograph of Auntie Patricia's family when the children were young teenagers. I always thought she had two girls, Maisie and young Margaret, but it seems from the photograph, and according to Maisie, that before Auntie Patricia was married out there, she also had a baby boy, and the tall young man alongside the two girls, was her son. I didn't know that," continued Ellie, "it was kept from me. The reason for them doing that was because, before I met your father... as young people might after the war..." Ellie paused trying to find the right words, "Patricia and your father met at a celebration party, so Maisie told me that her mother had explained to her, and they," she cleared her throat, "and they overreached themselves."

"What do you mean, Mum?" Brian asked, not quite getting her drift.

"They went to bed together." There, she had said it. "As a result, Auntie Patricia became pregnant and gave birth to Jack. That was why she went to Australia when she was eighteen, with my Auntie Lorna and Uncle George."

Brian was silent.

"So that means," he said, "that I have another cousin, or—" after a pause, "I have a half-brother! He must be older than I am if he was born before you met Dad. Good heavens! Fancy that!"

"I think he must be about five years older than you. Maisie said that he left home when he was eighteen," said his mother.

Brian was thoughtful for a while, and his mother didn't break the silence.

"I wish I had made an effort to come and meet Maisie, although at the time it would have been difficult to rearrange my timetable. If only Maisie had stayed in the town for longer – it was such a short visit," continued Brian. "You must have her address, Mum. I expect I have one of where they used to live. I would like to write to her and find out more about Jack."

Chapter 12

If Ellie thought Maisie was not taking note of the photographs on display in her front room, she was mistaken. As soon as Ellie left to make tea, Maisie was quietly on her feet looking intently at the photographs of Norman in his later life which were displayed on the top of a bookcase.

Maisie looked at her husband, John. He could see at once by her raised eyebrows and her look of astonishment, that she had seen something unexpected and surprising in the extreme. She went straight to the kitchen to help Ellie. Without a word she signalled to him to look at a photograph of Norman, sitting in a relaxed position in a garden chair with an open neck shirt and a broad smile on his face.

Maisie returned with the sandwiches and cakes and she smiled at Ellie as she followed with the tea trolley.

"Thank you so much for going to all this trouble," she said as she handed a cup of tea and a plate to John.

Nothing was said about the revelation each had had, it was too soon for either woman to voice her suspicions. Ellie kept silent, not wishing to embarrass her guests, and Maisie, did not wish to embarrass her hostess. Ellie would wait for her niece and her husband to leave before collecting her thoughts. Maisie would also wait to discuss her suspicions with husband John.

Maisie had made up her mind before she and John planned to call on Ellie, that she would avoid talking about Jack. It was an oversight that he appeared in the family photograph, and Maisie had been quick to say that Jack had left home when he was eighteen and that she had lost touch. It wasn't quite true, but convenient in the circumstances. Maisie was always very fond of Jack. She was aware that her mother and father had told him from an early age that David Wheatley was not his real father. It was obvious as Jack grew up, tall and good-looking that he was not a Wheatley. Better that he should know when he was young, than a suspicion rise in his mind as he grew to manhood, they had thought.

He nevertheless asked his mother who his real father was, Patricia always told him the truth, as she knew it, that she had been to a party after the war when peace was declared, and that she was silly enough to have sex with someone she didn't know. And that was as much as she divulged. Jack was never completely satisfied with her explanation.

He left home when he was eighteen to join the Police Force. He found he was growing away from his adopted father, and although he was fond of his mother and young sisters, he sought the company of young men out for independence and adventure, an inherited characteristic of both his parents. The world beckoned him. He did keep in touch with the family and went home on occasions at first, but in moving farther away, getting married and having a family of his own, his connection with his first family grew weaker. When his mother Patricia died, he returned home for her funeral. It was then that Maisie saw the older Jack that triggered off her recognition that he was very like Norman Hopeson, whom she had seen in the photographs. She was the only family member who had remembered her brother at Christmas time and answered his query as to how they were all keeping.

The years went by for him as they do for all who have time consuming jobs and families. Patricia's growing old and her increasing frailty did not fully register in Jack's busy life. His Mum would always be there for him when he had time to visit. Did he send her photographs of his family over the years? We hope he did, but we will never know for sure in this story.

Chapter 13

The Poplars
126 Brightling Road
PA2 FX9
U.K.

Dear Cousin Maisie,
Please accept my apologies for not meeting you on your recent visit to see my mother. I had meetings planned which could not be cancelled unfortunately. Thank you for going to see my mother, it gave her great pleasure to meet you and your husband John, and to receive news of her dear sister Patricia, and of her Auntie Lorna and Uncle George, all now gone from us.

I trust you were able to carry out your planned itinerary and that the weather was kind throughout your holiday here. Retirement is in my sights, and I too am looking forward to travelling abroad.

My mother mentioned to me that you had a half-brother, Jack, whom she had seen in the photographs, born before your mother married your father. I don't think my mother was aware of the fact, indeed, it came as a great surprise to her. No one in the family over here had ever mentioned it, which I found rather strange. Stranger still, is the fact that the photograph of Jack included in the one of your family, which you showed her, resembled her husband Norman, my father.

It is only natural that I ask if you were aware of Jack's parentage. Obviously, he was born before my mother's marriage. It is an intriguing story, I am very anxious to know if I have another cousin, and at the same time, a half-brother. As an only child myself, it is important for me to know the facts.

I therefore ask, is it possible that you are still in touch with your half-brother, and is he aware who his father was? I am very anxious to get in touch with him and I would be enormously grateful if you could let me know his whereabouts.

With best wishes to you and your family,

Your cousin,

Brian Hopeson.

PO 1006
Vicland, 97810
Australia
20.6

Hi Brian,

It was lovely to hear from you. We quite understood that you couldn't fit in a meeting with us. We loved meeting Auntie Ellie, she made us very welcome and was so keen to hear all our family news. She is an amazing lady.

Yes, it was a surprise for us to see the photographs of your father looking just like our Jack. Mother never really knew who his father was. I guess it was just one of those things, as they say.

Jack left home when he was eighteen to join the Police Force. I know he felt uncomfortable at times, as he would go off on his own when Dad's relations came. He did feel the odd one out as he was so tall, and not like the Wheatleys. He would be retired now. I know he married. I can't give you the last address I have for him. I am sorry that lately I have not been in touch with him. We moved house ourselves not long ago. I will look it out and send it to you, and I will try to get in touch with him and tell him what we have discovered.

All best wishes,

Love

Maisie and John.

When Ellie heard that Brian had received a letter from Maisie in answer to his request to be put in touch with Jack, she began to consider the possibility of his coming to England to meet Brian and herself. If Maisie informed him of who his father most likely was, he would be sure to want to fly over to meet his other family. Ellie realised that Maisie had seen Jack's likeness in her photographs of Norman, and like herself had been too shocked to say anything during her visit for fear of upsetting her. After all, it was a most embarrassing coincidence.

She found her world dominated by the news, she tried to imagine the circumstances which had led to Patricia becoming pregnant all those years ago. She found herself not surprised that Patricia had succumbed, as several young girls had at that time. That Norman had been the young teenager, she found more difficult to imagine. There it was, and the fact had to be accepted – she wouldn't dwell on it. Norman had been her loyal husband. He had devoted his life to his school and family. She was happy to face Jack with acceptance and affection.

However, Brian did not wait for Maisie to try and make contact with Jack. He wrote to Australia House and to the Police Force Records Office where they would know of Jack's whereabouts. He and his mother were impatient to receive news.

Maisie was just as eager to get in touch with Jack as her English relatives. She knew how much it would mean to him to know who his father was.

After receiving Brian's letter and immediately replying, she set about looking for her old address book, only recently put aside for a new one for the addresses of the people they were meeting, now that they had moved to a retirement area. There were boxes she had not opened since their move and she had not had time since John's retirement and their holiday, to open them up and find a home for everything.

Eventually, after much persistence, she retrieved the battered address book and found what she was looking for. She forwarded the address to Brian and at the same time she wrote to Jack.

Chapter 14

As it happened, the first communication to reach Jack Wheatley was from his sister, Maisie. Jack had not moved from his first home after his retirement. His family lived nearby, and his wife, Sue, was keen to stay close to them and be ready to have their grandchildren for sleepovers when their parents sought a much needed rest from a busy active household. Staying "put" for them was indispensable for the growing family.

Jack had been saddened over the years not to be able to tell his children who their grandfather was, even whether or not he was an Australian, he had come to believe that he was. It was hard for him to find no help from his birth certificate when "father unknown" was recorded. He was proud of his family, and in the days preceding his marriage, was lovingly grateful to his wife to be, for marrying him for who he was, and not being concerned about his background.

Such was the present lack of contact, Maisie had no phone number handy for Jack, and as for the internet, she and John had avoided getting involved. A priority letter, she thought, was best. She could take her time over her letter, giving Jack her new address and telephone number, for his expected immediate reply.

To say that Jack was surprised when Maisie's letter finally arrived, would be an understatement. Breakfast, always a leisurely affair, was over, the handwritten addressed letter was the first post to be opened. To hear from his sister was a pleasant surprise, but as he read on, his amazed silence and rapt attention brought an enquiry from his wife as to its contents. For a minute or two, Jack remained silent. The gnawing desire to know who his father was, which he had made every effort to control all his life, suddenly, in the blinking of an eye, was fulfilled. An unbelievable peace seemed to flow through him, as if he had put down a heavy load. He put his head in his hands and wept.

His reaction was of concern for his wife. Lifting his head he told her what the letter contained. Maisie's trip to England and her visit to see her Aunt Ellie had revealed who was, most likely, his father. It gave him the vital clue he sought, the inner satisfaction it gave him he could not describe, even to his wife. She was just happy to see him so elated. He could now do what he had always wanted to do – he would tell his children and grandchildren that his father was an Englishman and that the war was responsible for his being born to his mother, Patricia.

In her letter Maisie had explained how she had come to the conclusion that Ellie's husband, before his marriage, when still a teenager, had made his mother pregnant. That was the real reason for her emigrating to Australia.

Before Jack could contact Brian, a letter arrived from him, making obvious his delight at finding he had an elder brother. The long-awaited letter from Jack to Brian was also one of enormous pleasure at finding who his father was, and that he had a half-brother. A double joy he never expected to have at his age.

Maisie was delighted to be able to telephone her half-brother and reaffirm the news she had sent him with added information about their Aunt Ellie.

Jack's thoughts now centred on going to England to meet Ellie. Any information as to how to get there was eagerly sought from Maisie and her husband, John. They had hired a car, and had brought several maps and pamphlets back home with them. It was all a good reason for meeting up. A weekend visit to Maisie's was arranged. It was an exciting time for the retired couples. Maisie and John busied themselves organising accommodation for their guests, Jack and Sue prepared to help with food for catering for their visit.

Chapter 15

There was a considerable amount of planning to be done for Ellie and Brian when finally the date for the visit of Jack and his wife had been chosen.

It would be impossible for Ellie to entertain them at her home, even though she had room. Gone were the days when energy was taken for granted, and one did not have to think about it sagging and running out of steam. Being animated in conversation could be draining.

Brian was sure Jack would want to make the most of his visit and see something of the country as Maisie and John had done, although this time they would want to spend longer with their new family.

In the end, Brian was freeing himself from his work to enable him to meet and welcome his brother and his wife at the airport and drive them to his home, where they could make it a base from which to travel wherever they wished. There they could meet his family. When they had recovered and settled after the journey, he would drive them down to see Ellie for a day, returning again at the end of their time in England.

Plans were made via email this time, enabling details to be decided upon quickly. The two men were now familiar with each other and eager to meet each other face to face. So, with willing consent they arranged to use Skype and link up on their computers to introduce themselves. It would make recognition and greeting at the airport so much easier. Ellie was not included in this, the arrangement would have been too complicated.

It was a thoughtful time for Ellie, she wondered how many were involved in knowing of Patricia's pregnancy. She felt the knowledge here in this country must have been limited to her parents and to her Aunt Lorna and Uncle George. The Hopesons would not have known. She wondered what contact there had been with the Wheatleys. It all seemed so confusing. One thing was clear, that she knew nothing of Jack until Maisie's visit. Perhaps she really should leave it at that. When human behaviour deviated from the natural and normal, there were bound to be repercussions which caused ripples. Thankfully, this time there could be a happy ending. Brian would have a brother, as near as normally possible, Ellie would be pleased about it, as she had always wanted to have another child.

Because Brian had been an only one, Ellie, quite a long time ago, had made her will totally in Brian's favour. She had told him that it was her wish that he should help his two children from her legacy, should there be any inheritance. She was quite realistic about her future, but she hoped to 'wind down' gently, as she put it. Her wants had been very few recently, her friends were unable to take holidays with her, as in days of yore. She remembered lovely times with them and was thankful.

Her thoughts returned to the question of whether or not she should include Jack in her legacy. Would he be entitled to a half share as Norman's son? She felt that she should consult her solicitor son. Jack, too, had a family. She felt she must come to a decision quickly and not let the subject play on her mind – it only disturbed her sleep.

In fact, after thinking about it for a while, she decided she would amend her will, so that a modest amount be left to Jack, without mentioning it to Brian. Her son had worked hard all his life and was not in need, neither, it seemed was Jack. He had also served his community well in the Police Force, and retired with a pension. The matter was settled in her mind. It pleased her to think Norman would approve – she felt she had done the right thing. She would wait patiently for them, trying not to get too excited, sending her blood pressure up. Her helper, Dorothy, would make sure the house was clean and presentable for another visit from her Australian visitors, with some welcoming flowers.

The importance of the occasion, wanting to be a good hostess, encouraged Ellie to call on her neighbour Bea.

Starting with a cautious opening, Ellie said, "Bea, I hope I am not disturbing you, but I wonder if I could ask a favour of you."

"Of course you can, come in," replied Bea without hesitation and offering a hand to Ellie over her threshold.

Ellie's heart warmed to her neighbour's welcome. She felt quite comfortable in asking for her help in preparing tea for her other Australian visitors. She explained that her niece Maisie had returned to Australia with glowing reports of her visit, and now her recently retired brother and his wife had decided to come for a similar visit, combining touring to the well-known sites and visiting relatives. Nothing was said relating to the filial discovery. She was pleased and relieved when Bea said that she was only too willing to help Ellie this time.

Chapter 16

I've been here before, thought Ellie, as she sat waiting in the lounge, dressed in her best 'Sunday go to meeting' clothes.

The day had arrived. The plan had been carefully explained to her by Brian over the telephone. Jack and Sue would drive down with him in time for introductions, to be followed, after a short time, by lunch out at a local hotel. After coffee in the lounge there, they would return to spend the afternoon with her. She had begged for a short rest on returning, she felt sure she would need to close her eyes and sit quietly, then she would feel refreshed for an afternoon with her guests.

Ellie's recent hunt to unearth an old album Norman had kept of photographs of his family, Brian, Jack and Sue could look through while she rested. She thought it doubtful that Brian had ever seen them, they were old black and white photographs going back to the nineteen thirties.

She had rested for most of the morning. Bea had arrived for a cup of coffee, she arrived early to make sure there was time to visit the local shop should something have been forgotten. With Ellie's forward planning it was not necessary. Quietly and without a rush, sandwiches were made and covered, together with a selection of cakes. Ellie regretted that she could not have made the cakes herself, but there it was. There was nothing more to be done. She thanked Bea and sat in her chair to await their arrival.

All in good time, almost to the minute, she heard Brian's key in the door.

"We are here, Mum," came his voice loud and clear.

"Come through," she answered, trying to steady her voice which despite herself was full of emotion.

Ellie rose from her chair carefully, and made her way further into the room. She waited for her son and her Australian guests, listening to her son's quiet welcoming and directing them as to where they should hang their coats. It was only April and still chilly.

But suddenly, she found herself overcome with nervousness. She returned to her chair to steady herself, at the last minute she felt quite unprepared to meet Jack. She couldn't stand and greet her guests as she had planned to do.

Always in control and sensible, she found herself on the verge of tears at the prospect of seeing someone resembling her husband Norman. She found herself asking for strength from somewhere, in a pleading inner voice.

Then Brian came through the door smiling, he came over to where she sat and kissed her.

"Jack is a bit nervous at meeting you," he said. "He is still taking off his coat and Sue is waiting for him." Then he returned to the hall.

That makes two of us, thought Ellie. *I must try to be welcoming*. And summoning her strength, she stood up, still holding the chair for support.

Brian came in and immediately was at his mother's side taking her arm.

"Here they are, Mum, This is Jack and Sue."

Jack came slowly towards Ellie and took her hand kissing it gently. Sue followed and quietly greeted her.

Ellie found herself momentarily at a loss for words as she looked intently at this distinguished tall elderly gentleman, so obviously a member of the Hopeson family.

"Do sit down," she said, "and let me look at you." There was a pause, and Jack did not interrupt. "I can see your mother and Norman." There was another pause, and then she continued more confidently, "I am so pleased to meet you and Sue. You know, Jack," she continued, pointing to the empty armchairs, "I did not know that my sister had a son. When these things happened, I was still young. My parents looked upon it as a misfortune and something to be hidden, the irregularity of war time was blamed. I am so pleased to have lived to meet you. I am ninety-one, you know."

"We are so pleased to meet you and Brian," said Sue eagerly. "Maisie told us how wonderful you are living on your own and able to look after yourself. It is lovely here," she said looking admiringly at the attractive lounge. "Do you have help to do the hard work?"

And so thankfully, the ice was broken and the questions and answers flowed between them. Ellie sensed that Jack and Brian had become as brothers, long lost, and were getting to know each other as quickly as they could. Ellie appreciated Sue's gentle quiet approach, and she was conscious that Sue was the age of the daughter she had never had.

They prepared to leave again for lunch at the hotel Brian had chosen, knowing that it was one where his mother had been before, and where she would feel comfortable.

Her initial nervousness gone, Ellie relaxed and enjoyed her meal interspersed with moments of conversation. Every now and again she glanced at Jack when he was engaged in eating his meal. Expressions were studied as he turned to the right, then to the left, the serious look, the look of an inner happiness with a quiet smile. And that other expression she could not quite place.

Sue struck the right note with Ellie, relating her background as a third generation Australian. She supposed that she too had relations in the United Kingdom, if she traced her ancestry. She wasn't really interested in that she said.

Everyone said they had enjoyed the meal, which pleased Brian. He was thanked for his hospitality, and the party moved away to enjoy coffee in the hotel lounge.

Brian sensed his mother had become quiet and had ceased to be joining in the conversation so eagerly. It was time to return to her home.

Chapter 17

On reaching her home, Ellie retired to her bedroom. She could hear the buzz of conversation downstairs and imagined them looking through the old photograph album. It was always entertaining to see the fashions of the thirties, forties and fifties, and the seaside pleasures of those days just before and after the war. There were one or two of Norman and his brother as babies, and some of their mother with the boys as toddlers, and later on at school age, when they were on holiday. There was one of Norman's father in the uniform of the Civil Defence taken during the war. At the back of the album were some of the boys, Norman in the uniform of the Army Cadets when he was sixteen and at school, and one of his brothers in the uniform of a Sea Cadet. Ellie tried hard to recall Norman's brother's name, but she could not.

She must have dropped off to sleep, for waking and looking at her bedside clock, she realised that over an hour had passed. The house was silent. She tidied herself and made her way downstairs. She entered her front lounge and found Jack asleep in an armchair, there was no sign of Brian and Sue. She looked intently at Jack, relaxed and at ease. It was many years since her husband had died, the photographs of him that she had showed him younger than the age Jack was now. Norman wasn't so grey as Jack, nor as lined, nevertheless Jack was a Hopeson.

The front door opened and Brian was heard talking to Sue. They came into the lounge still wearing their outdoor clothes. Brian helped Sue remove hers and carried them into the hall.

"Fancy Jack still asleep," she said softly. "He didn't have a very good night. All this excitement I think," she added with a smile. "We didn't want to disturb him, so Brian took me to see the park."

The sound of their voices was enough for Jack to open his eyes, he apologised for going to sleep, but said he felt refreshed and ready for a cup of tea.

Ellie also felt refreshed after her sleep and went quickly into the kitchen, followed by Sue, willing to help transport the well-prepared afternoon tea into the front lounge on a trolley.

"Did you enjoy looking at the old family photos?" Ellie asked them when they were sitting down, plates on lap and teacups safely deposited on her seldom used nest of tables.

"I found them fascinating," replied Jack. "I feel now as if I belong to the family as well. To see my grandparents was very moving for me. I didn't realise that my father had a brother. I see he was a Sea Cadet."

"Oh yes," said Ellie. "For the life of me, I cannot remember his name at the moment. He joined the Merchant Navy and was hardly ever at home. I remember Norman saying that his parents were disappointed that they saw him so rarely. He never married and died abroad."

"Perhaps he had a wife in every port," said Sue innocently.

"Is his name written on the back of the photograph anywhere?" asked Ellie, feeling she should know more about him, his name at least.

"It was very faint," said Brian, "it could have been 'Jim'. I can't remember having met him, but I suppose I did when I was very young."

Ellie wracked her brain, but could not remember anything.

The conversation centred on Jack and Sue's coming holiday plans. Brian was accompanying them for a few days before his work called him back. Then they would be free to explore the country on their own. Before they returned to Australia they would meet up with Brian's family before coming to say 'good bye' to Ellie, another lunch out and away they would go.

So 'good byes' this time were not final. It made it easier for Ellie.

Hardly had the car driven off down the road, then Bea was out on the pavement.

"Don't you attempt to clear away, Ellie," she said in a stern voice.

"I will help you," Ellie replied firmly.

Chapter 18

Ellie noticed how alive Brian had become in Jack's company, wanting to know about his work in the Australian Police Force as regards their work in the courts there, for Brian, as a solicitor, was often involved with the court here. They had much in common. Each was interested in the other's family, for they knew that their children would be interested in their overseas cousins. Jack's family would want to know every detail about the Hopesons. Although they all grew up with the name, Wheatley, they knew it was a name by adoption. They would know that their maternal grandfather and grandmother were called Sparkes. It made an interesting family tree. Jack would want to trace his ancestry, he had time to do so now.

What a mix of genes we have, thought Ellie, as she sat and pondered over the afternoon conversations. Thinking of the Hopeson family she tried to fill in the blank she had concerning Norman's brother. By the time she met Norman, his brother was away finishing his degree at university. She knew he was studying engineering and was aiming to become a ship's engineer. She was aware that after university he did not spend much time at home. Ellie tried to remember when they last met, but it was so long ago now that her memory was very faint where he was concerned. Odd, she thought, that Patricia became distant to her, and Norman's brother didn't keep in close contact with him. It was all before the internet and iPad days, and not everyone was good at keeping up a correspondence. Ellie's thoughts recalled a remark that Sue had made when she told them that Norman's brother had never married, to their knowledge anyway. "A wife in every port," Sue had said.

Ellie wondered if Patricia had met Norman's brother, after all, they were a local family.

A thought came suddenly to her mind. What if Jack was the son of Norman's brother? She had always found it hard to understand Patricia's pregnancy as the result of Norman's behaviour with her sister, but had accepted it, and believed that Brian and Jack were half-brothers. Now there was an element of doubt in her mind, but in the end, it would still mean that the men were cousins. There was no way she was going to disturb the relationship, whatever the truth of the matter, and her plan to include Jack in her will would stand. If she didn't do it for Norman, she would do it for Patricia. It would be a bond between Jack and Brian.

She was sure her son had been delighted to have found a family member to fill a gap in his life. And she knew from Sue, that knowing his real Hopeson family had brought Jack immense satisfaction. It was her decision to keep her feelings to herself. Life is a matter of choices, she decided, we were all responsible for our own actions and there was great satisfaction in doing the right thing. She could sleep without thoughts of the past going round and round in her mind. She wanted to enjoy the last years, or maybe just days, of her life, thinking well of her family and being thankful for them all.

She turned on her light and drew her curtains. She felt sure that she would sleep well, and decided to go straight to bed. No watching the television tonight, and she was sure that her dreams would be sweet ones.